The Impressionists
COLORING BOOK

With paintings selected and redrawn by Andy Nelson

Culpepper Press

MINNEAPOLIS

A Note to Parents, Grandparents, and Friends of Children...

If you're like me, your childhood exposure to art consisted of Norman Rockwell calendars, Walt Disney comics, and perhaps a Currier & Ives coffee table book that had been given to your parents as a wedding gift. How wonderful that you can introduce the Impressionists to the important youngsters in your life through *The Impressionists Coloring Book*!

These Impressionist (and post-Impressionist) images were selected for their familiarity and for their ability to be translated into line drawings suitable for coloring. A variety of representative subjects were chosen to give the reader a well-rounded introduction to Impressionism. The selections also have varying degrees of "coloring complexity."

Here are some hints that may make coloring more enjoyable:

1. Don't feel compelled to color in every separate little space with a different color. Many of the lines are there simply to help retain a resemblance to the original painting. (Folds in clothing are a good example of this.) If you can't figure out an area, go with your gut feeling, your instinct, your first "impression."

2. Be bold and inventive in your colors. Always think as the Impressionists did—think light and shadow. Remember, there are flowers all over the place! In fields, on dresses, in hats, in hair, on hands, in vases, everywhere!

3. Experiment with different color media and techniques. Vary the strokes and patterns of your crayons. Try coloring entirely with dots like Seurat. Try colored pencils or fine point markers for greater detail. Remove the pages to paint with watercolor or pastels. Break up larger solid areas into colorful patches of light and dark, as the Impressionists often did.

4. Neatness does not count.

5. The empty borders on left-hand pages are for you to copy the drawing or draw your own original compositions of similar subjects in your life. On these pages you will also find the artist's name, title and date of the work, current owner, size of original by height and width, and a brief historic note.

6. Finally, go to the library to look at the paintings in color before you begin. Or, better yet, color your "masterpiece" and then seek out a picture of the original painting to compare your "impressions."

We hope you will enjoy this book, that you will reacquaint yourself with the Impressionists, and that you will always take the time to encourage a child to draw, color, and paint. Thank you. —*Andy Nelson*

About the artist:

ANDY NELSON is a Minnesota artist whose work includes portraits, drawings, paintings, prints and murals. He is the illustrator for the Minneapolis Review of Baseball. His last book was *A is for At Bat, A Baseball Primer*, an illustrated baseball ABCs also published by Culpepper Press. Andy holds degrees in studio art, art history, and education.

———————

For my daughters, Bethany and Shannon.

———————

Cover painting: Jean-Auguste Renoir, The Luncheon of the Boating Party.
Reproduced by permission of The Phillips Collection, Washington, D.C.

ISBN 0-939636-06-6   10 9 8 7 6 5 4 3 2 1

CULPEPPER PRESS
2901 Fourth St. SE
Minneapolis, Minnesota 55414
Culpepper Press books are available to organizations in quantity. Write for information.

Introduction

In France in the first half of the 1800s ambitious artists showed their paintings in *salons* — very formal exhibits of paintings approved by both the state and the public. Salons were administered and juried by officials from special academies of art. Acceptance by the salon was the only road to a successful career in art. Paintings which did not bear a stamp of association from an accredited art academy stood little chance of being accepted for display. Each salon was flooded by 2,000 or more artists submitting 5,000 or more paintings. The judges stamped two-thirds them on the back with the word *REJECT* in big red letters. Not only did this stamp keep the work out of the salon, but it also ensured that its future sale was severely limited.

Around 1860, a group of young men and women from Paris and the surrounding countryside met for the first time at these salons and academies. These young painters were united in their rejecting of the stifling atmosphere of official art and their desire to bring their work before the public. Paris — the political, social and art capitol of the world — was the place to do this. At first these artists gathered informally in bars, cafes and homes. They exhibited for the first time as a group in 1874, at which time an art critic mockingly labeled them as mere "impressionists." The artists, however, accepted this title with pride and exhibited six more times in the next dozen years.

The Impressionists sought a truer representation of nature and humanity's interrelationship with it. Desiring more direct contact with their subjects, they abandoned their studios for open-air painting, stretching smaller canvases that could be easily tucked under an arm. Newly manufactured commercial paints, brighter and bolder than older colors, now came in convenient little tubes, which also made outdoor painting easier. These artists also rebelled against the tiny, smooth brushstrokes and finicky modeling of the style favored by the salons and academies. Their new brush strokes reflected the rapidity with which they attacked their canvases. Color and form became more important to them than line. Above all, they celebrated light as the primary subject of their paintings. Impressionists also rejected the assumption that a painting's subject had to have great literary value. Their subjects reflected the warmth of everyday life. They ad- monished "Paint what you see, not what you know!" Many of their compositions were influenced by the odd perspectives and flat colors of Japanese prints.

Of the 17 artists represented in this book, 14 were French, two were American, one was English and one was Dutch. Two were women. Eight came from very wealthy backgrounds, seven came from the middle-class, and two were born to poor families. By the 1880s, "Impressionism" as a formal group was disbanding: most of the artists were in their-mid 40s and mid-50s and were pursuing more individualistic careers. But this loosely organized group — at first misunderstood, reviled, and ignored by the public, critics, and collectors — had by then seen their new vision of painting embraced by art lovers. Some eventually earned financial and critical success within their own lifetimes. All told, they changed the history of art as no group of artists had done before. The Impressionists planted the seeds of modern art, and today Impressionist paintings are the most popular in the world.

This coloring book includes works by the following artists:

Edouard Manet (1832-1883)
Claude Monet (1840-1926)
Pierre-Auguste Renoir (1841-1919)
Edgar Degas (1834-1917)
Mary Cassatt (1845-1926)
Berthe Morisot (1841-1895)
Camille Pissarro (1830-1903)
Frédéric Bazille (1841-1870)
Alfred Sisley (1839-1899)
Gustave Caillebotte (1848-1894)
James McNeill Whistler (1834-1903)
Paul Cézanne (1839-1906)
George Seurat (1859-1891)
Paul Signac (1863-1935)
Vincent van Gogh (1853-1890)
Paul Gauguin (1848-1903)
Henri de Toulouse-Lautrec (1864-1901)

We encourage you to learn more about the art of the Impressionists at your local library.

Edouard Manet
ARGENTEUIL, 1874
Musee des Beaux Arts, Tournai, Belgium (59x52 in.)

Manet's life was easy-going and well-off, but he was dissatisfied to have never achieved the social recognition he so desperately craved. This work was rejected by the Salon in 1876.

Edouard Manet
THE EXECUTION OF THE EMPEROR MAXIMILIAN, 1867
The National Gallery, London (75x63 in.)

Born to a family of governmental ministers and diplomats, Manet had originally studied law and was a naval officer. He later enlisted as a lieutenant during the Franco-Prussian War.

Edouard Manet
LUNCH IN THE STUDIO, 1868-69
Neue Staatsgalerie, Munich (47x61 in.)

Unlike other Impressionists, Manet steadfastly refused to eliminate the color
black from his painting palette. More so than the others, his aesthetic beliefs
remained entwined with the traditional past.

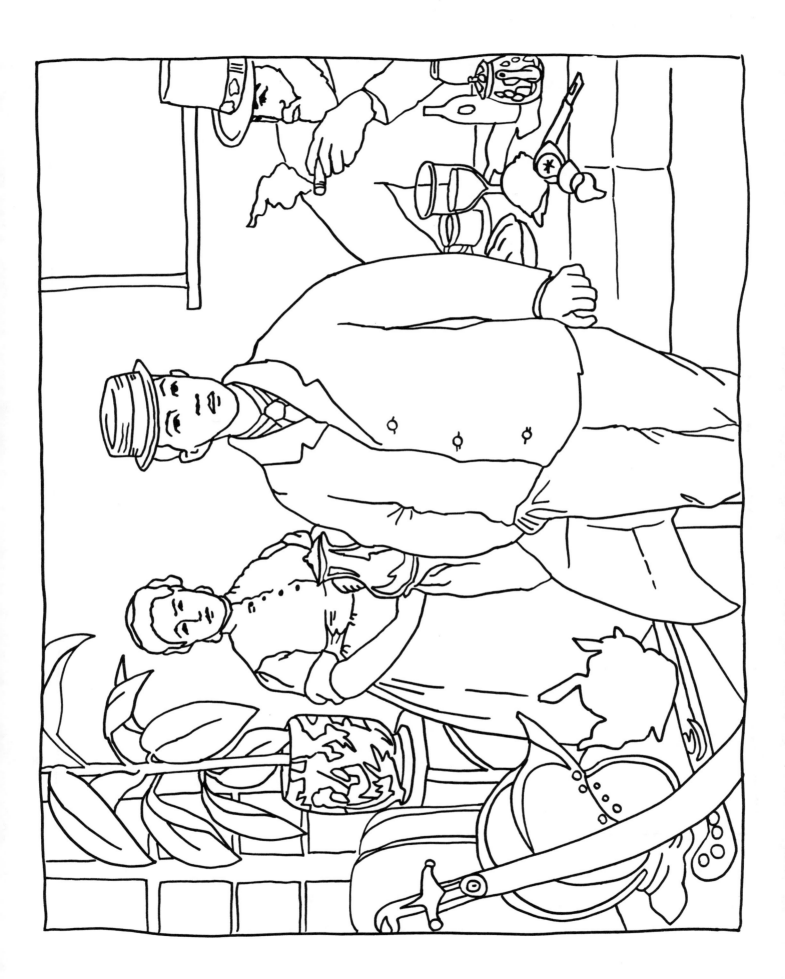

Edouard Manet
GARE ST.-LAZARE (Le Chemin de Fer), 1873
National Gallery of Art, Washington, D.C. (37x45 in.)

This painting was accepted by the Salon in 1873. The model for this mother was
the same one who had modeled for his previously rejected "Olympia" and "Picnic
on the Grass."

Edouard Manet
BAR AT THE FOLIES-BERGERE, 1881-82
Courtlauld Institute Galleries, London (38x51 in.)

This was one of Manet's last works, painted the year before he died at age 51.
Ironically, it earned him a posthumously bestowed Legion of Honor, an award he
had coveted all his life.

Claude Monet
THE BEACH AT TROUVILLE, 1870
The National Gallery, London (15x18 in.)

The son of shopkeepers, Monet lived most of his life in debt. So poor was he that
his wife, Camille, modeled for all the figures in many of his paintings.

Claude Monet
WOMEN IN THE GARDEN, 1866-67
Louvre, Paris (100x80 in.)

Once, when Monet was in need, his wealthy best friend Bazille bought this painting for 2,500 francs. As usual, Monet's wife modeled for all the women in this
composition.

Claude Monet
A FIELD OF POPPIES, 1873
Louvre, Paris (20x26 in.)

Nothing about an Impressionist landscape was to be picturesque. All that mattered was the impression of nature: light was always the real subject of the painting.

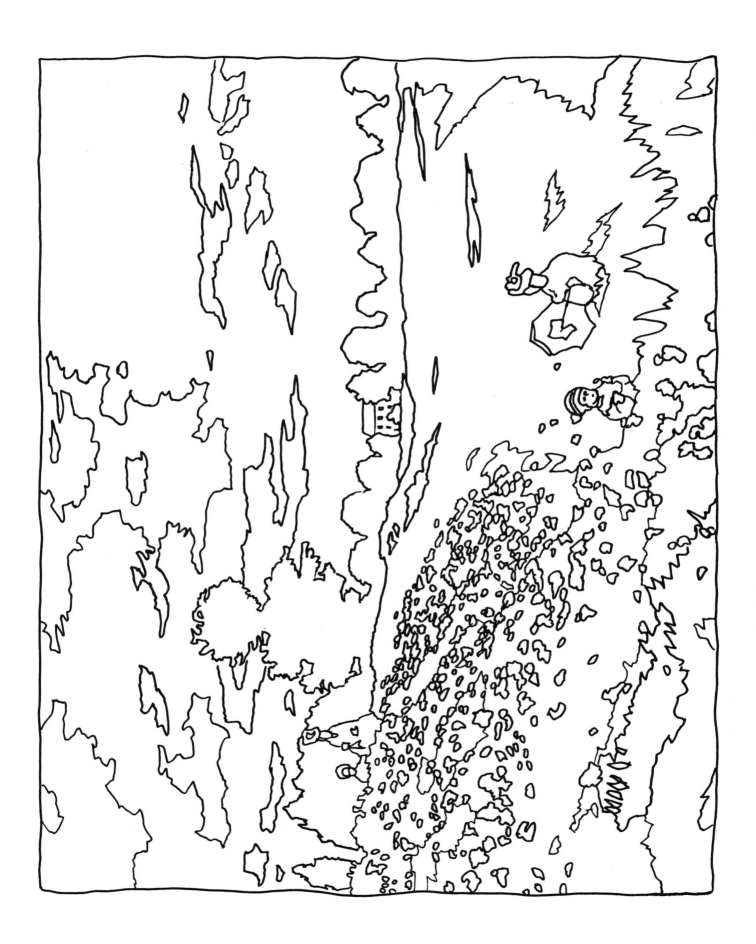

Claude Monet
LA JAPONAISE, 1876
Museum of Fine Arts, Boston (91x56 in.)

European trade with the Orient was peaking, and with his friends Monet was greatly influenced by Japanese art. Many of the Impressionists collected Japanese prints, fans, and kimonos.

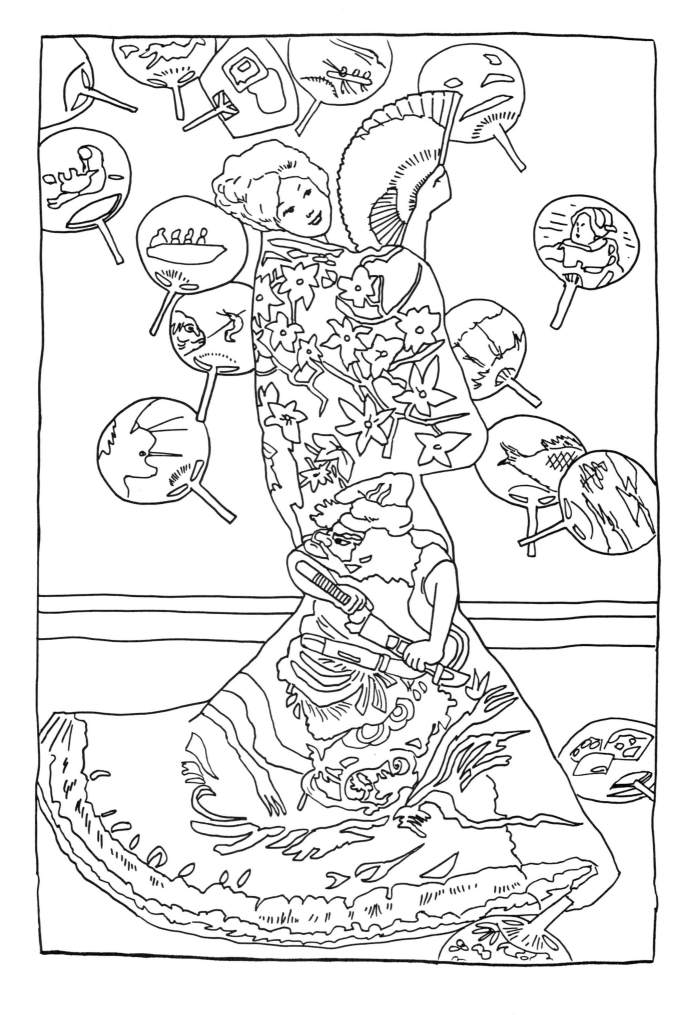

Pierre-Auguste Renoir
THE CLOWN, 1868
Rijksmuseum Kroller-Muller, Otterlo (76x51 in.)

The clown has been a favorite subject of painters ever since Renoir painted this lifesize portrait. Others, especially Degas, Seurat, and Toulouse-Lautrec, also painted clowns and circus performers.

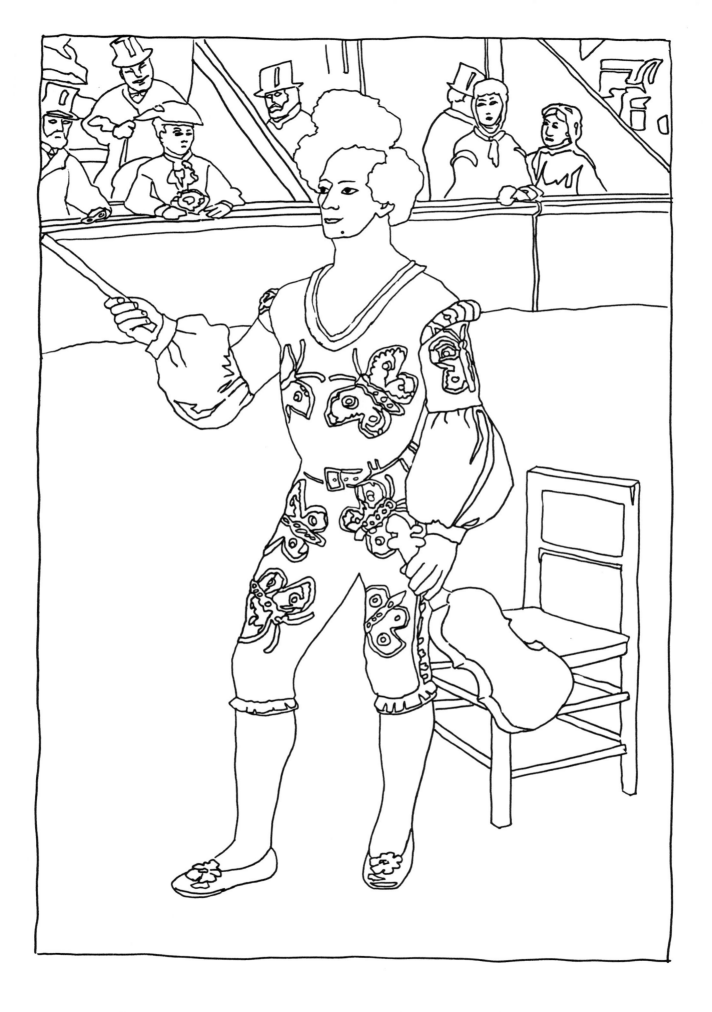

Pierre-Auguste Renoir
LES PARAPLUIES
The National Gallery, London

The son of a poor tailor, Renoir was determined to become a painter, but not to burden his impoverished family. He earned his first paychecks as a painter of chinaware vases.

Pierre-Auguste Renoir
ON THE TERRACE, 1881
Chicago Institute of Art (40x32 in.)

Renoir believed that because his pictures were pleasant and pretty, people were quick to dismiss him as a minor painter. However, he refused to paint tiresome subjects.

Pierre-Auguste Renoir
LUNCHEON OF THE BOATING PARTY, 1881
Phillips Collection, Washington, D.C. (51x68 in.)

Renoir was at the height of his success when he painted this. His friends were the models: his future wife cuddles the dog; the painter and collector Caillebotte is seated at right.

Pierre-Auguste Renoir
GIRL WITH A HOOP, 1885
National Gallery of Art, Washington, D.C. (50x30 in.)

In his later years, severe rheumatism compelled Renoir to work from a wheel-chair, with brushes strapped to his hand. But always his innate good humor sustained him.

Edgar Degas
DANCERS IN REPOSE
Private Collection

From aristocratic lineage, Degas forsook the study of law for art, as did Manet and Cézanne. Degas was extremely intelligent, logical, belligerent, and difficult to get along with.

Edgar Degas
JOCKEYS IN THE RAIN, c. 1881
Burrell Collection, Glasgow (18x25 in.)

Degas abhorred the label "Impressionist," preferring instead to call himself a "Realist." His subjects—theater, ballet, racehorses, and working women—were all completely novel.

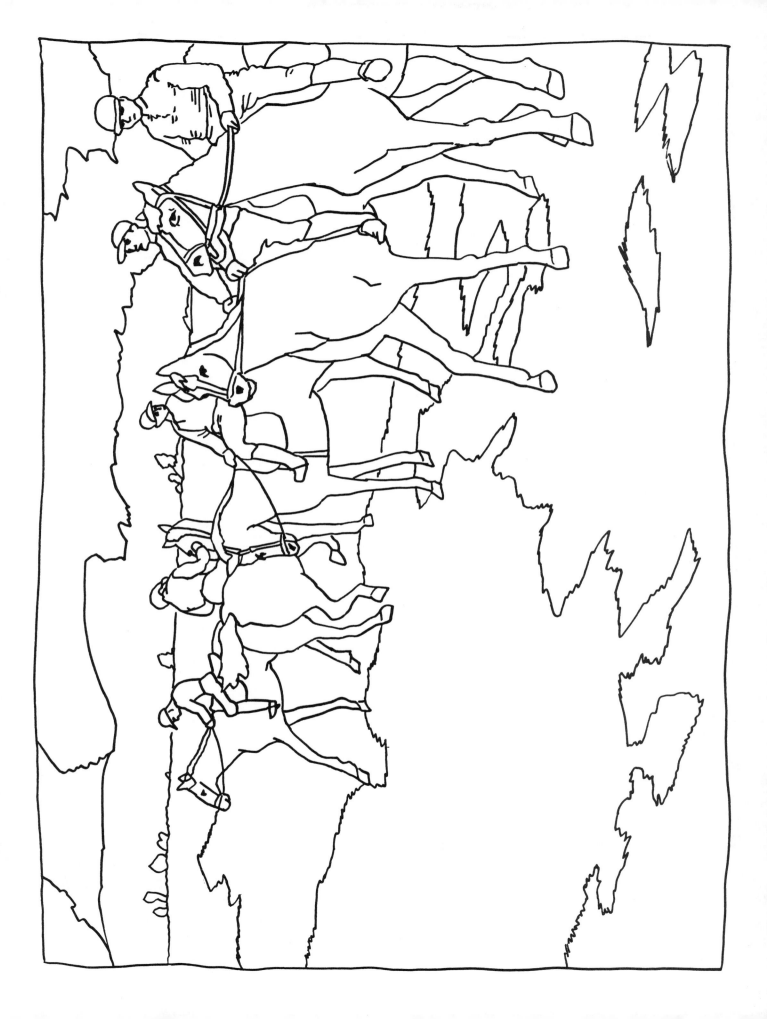

Edgar Degas
MISS LALA AT THE CIRCUS FERNANDO, 1879
The National Gallery, London (46x30 in.)

Unlike his Impressionist friends, Degas did not believe in open-air painting, nor in direct impressions. "My art is in no way spontaneous; it is entirely contrived," he once said.

Edgar Degas
THE MILLINERY SHOP, c. 1882
Chicago Institute of Art (39x43 in.)

Although women were his most common subject, Degas' only true retreat from
misogyny was his deep friendship with the American painter Mary Cassatt.

Edgar Degas
WOMAN IRONING, 1882
National Gallery of Art, Washington, D.C. (32x26 in.)

As his eyesight failed, Degas' work became less dependent on line and more on colorful strokes and forms. Threatened with blindness by age 50, he gave up pastels for sculpture.

Mary Cassatt
A CUP OF TEA, 1880
Museum of Fine Arts, Boston (26x36 in.)

Cassatt was born into a Pittsburgh banking family who sent her to study art in Europe when she was 23. This painting typifies her elegant social life outside of her art.

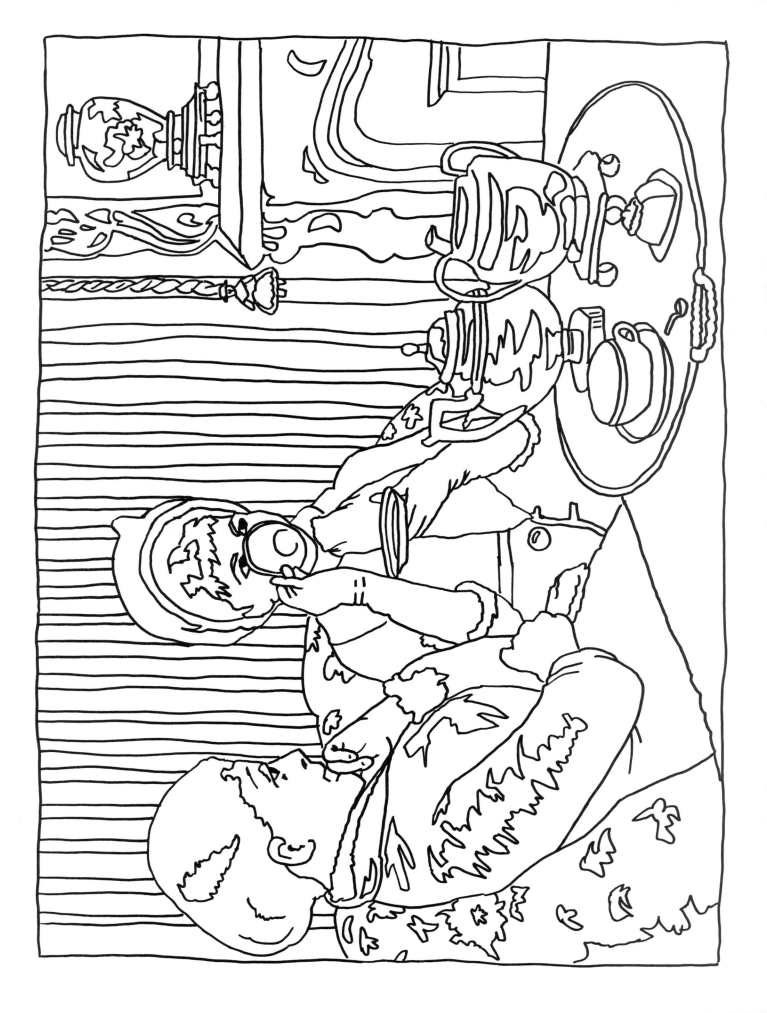

Mary Cassatt
THE BOATING PARTY, 1893-94
National Gallery of Art, Washington, D.C. (36x46 in.)
Cassatt, the greatest artist since Raphael to celebrate motherhood, regretted
never having been a mother herself.

Mary Cassatt
TWO CHILDREN AT THE SEASHORE, 1884
National Gallery of Art, Washington, D.C. (38x29 in.)

Cassatt contributed greatly to the introduction of Impressionist works to her American friends. She died, nearly blind, at age 81 in 1926 in her adopted home-land of France.

Berthe Morisot
THE BALCONY, 1872
Ittleson Collection, New York (24x20 in.)

Of bourgeois background, Morisot was encouraged in her art by her brother-in-law, Manet. She was included in the first Impressionist exhibit in 1874.

Camille Pissarro
JALLAIS HILL, PONTOISE, 1867
Metropolitan Museum of Art, New York (34x45 in.)

Pissarro was the oldest of the group. He was the great encourager of young painters. Gauguin, Signac, Seurat, van Gogh, and particularly Cézanne, benefitted
from his kindness.

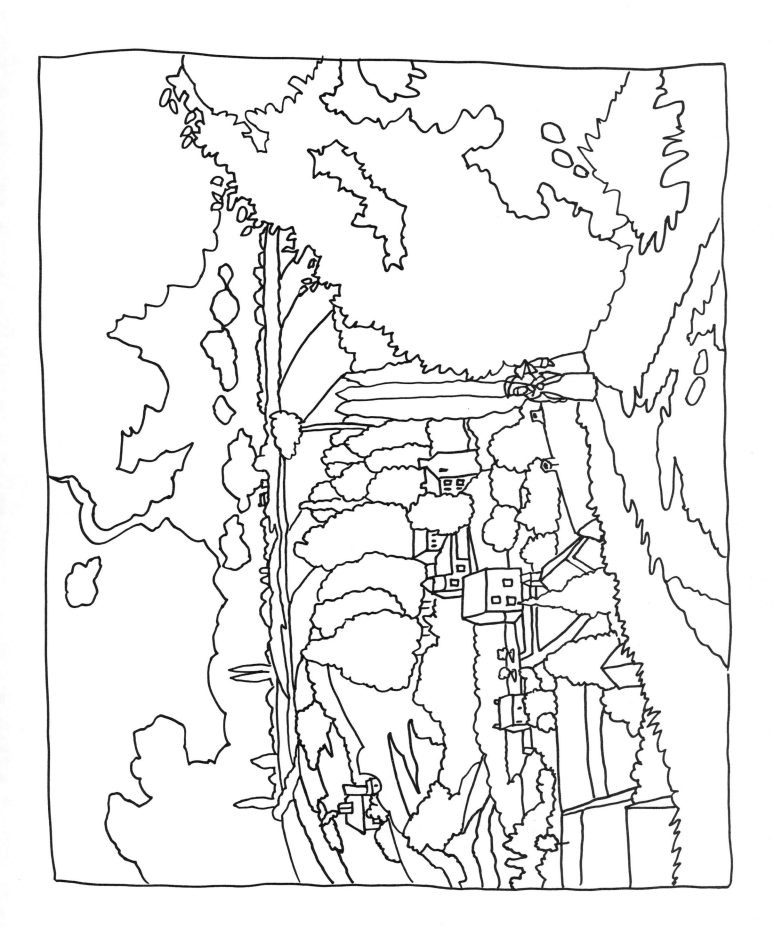

Camille Pissarro
GRAY MORNING AT ROUEN, 1898
Private Collection, Paris (32x26 in.)

During the Franco-Prussian War, Pissarro became a refugee. He returned to a studio ransacked by Prussians who had destroyed 1,500 of his paintings.

Frédéric Bazille
PORTRAIT OF RENOIR, 1867
Musee des Beaux Arts, Algiers (25x20 in.)

Born into the fashionable upper-class, Bazille was always ready to help his less fortunate painter friends. He was the first to envision a society of friends who would exhibit their work.

Frédéric Bazille
BATHERS (Scene d'Ete), 1869
Fogg Art Museum, Harvard University (62x62 in.)

A generous and personable man, Bazille studied medicine as well as art. His works are few. He enlisted as a *Zouave* in the Franco-Prussian War and was killed in battle at age 29.

Alfred Sisley (1839-1899)
VIEW OF THE SEVRES ROAD, 1873
Musee D'Orsay, Paris

Sisley was born of British parents but lived his entire life in France. Financially ruined by the death of his father, Sisley nevertheless continued to pursue a painting career.

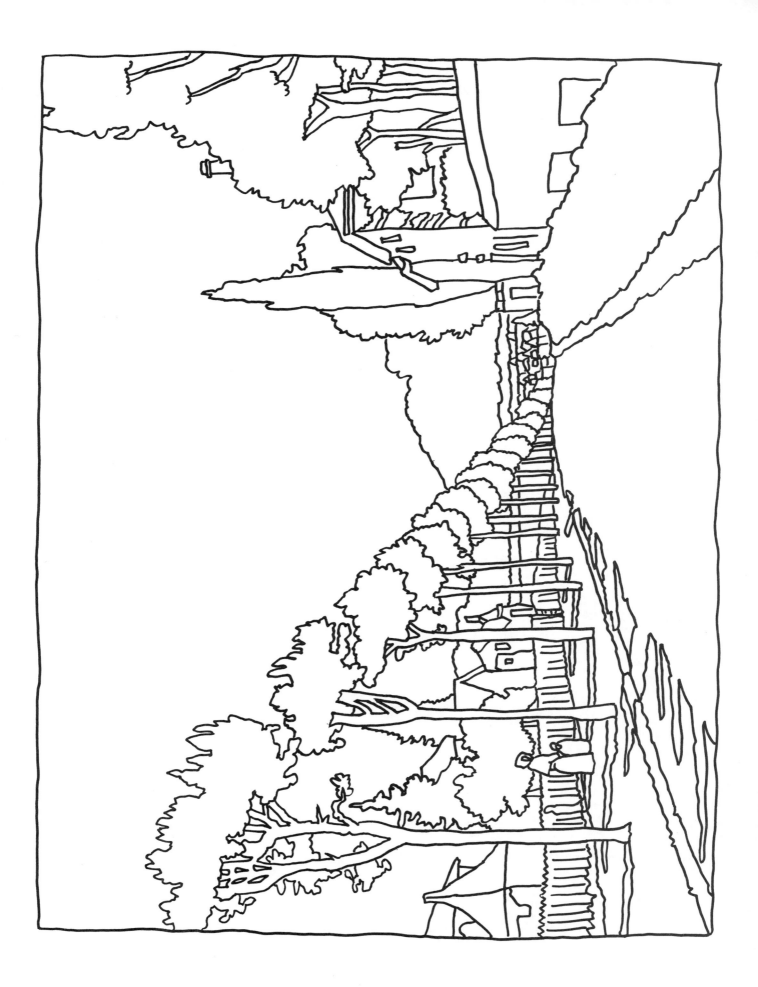

Alfred Sisley
THE BRIDGE AT VILLENEUVE-LA-GARENNE, 1872
Metropolitan Museum of Art, New York (19x26 in.)

Sisley's works were practically unknown among his generation and are often infused with melancholy. He was withdrawn and irritable, and died of throat cancer at age 60.

Gustave Caillebotte
STREET IN PARIS, A RAINY DAY, 1887
Chicago Institute of Art (84x109 in.)

A timid and reserved bachelor, easily discouraged, Caillebotte abandoned painting for marine engineering. But he bought many of his friends "unsalable" works and left them to the Louvre.

James Abbott McNeill Whistler
CAPRICE IN PURPLE AND GOLD, NO. 2:
THE GOLDEN SCREEN, 1864
Freer Gallery of Art, Washington, D.C. (20x27 in.)

An American who befriended Degas and Manet, Whistler lived most of his life in London, where he achieved great honor and reward as a portrait painter and etcher.

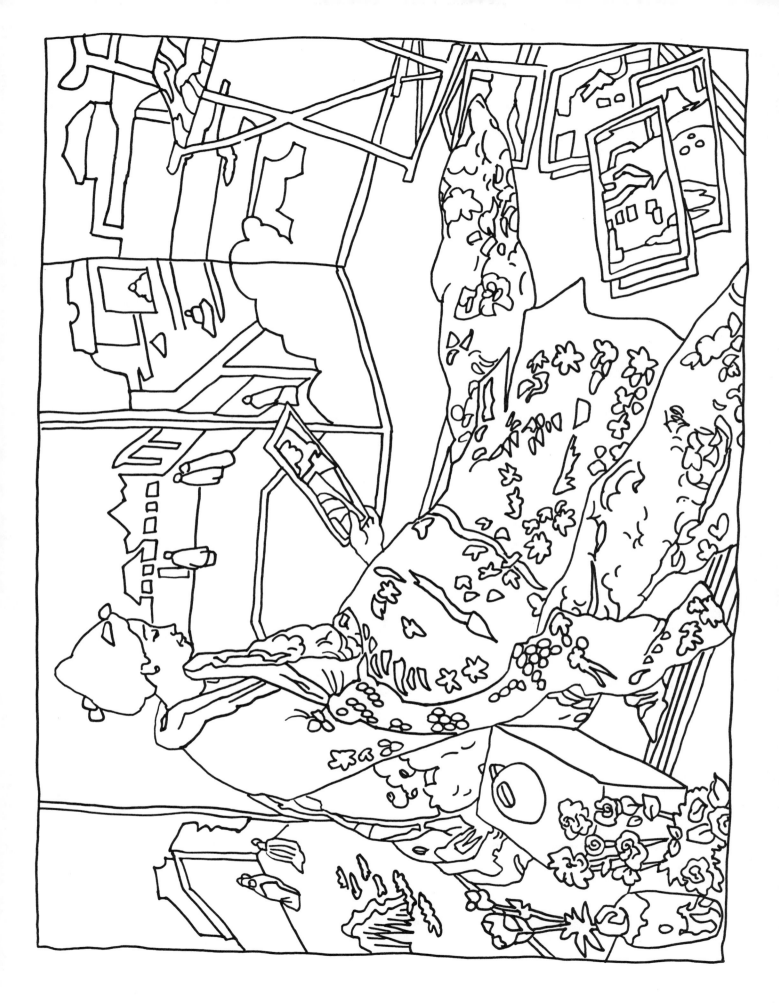

Paul Cézanne
CARDPLAYERS, 1890-92
Metropolitan Museum of Art, New York (25x32 in.)

Born of wealthy banker parents, Cézanne's shy and modest nature was often
misinterpreted as fierceness. Big city life oppressed him; he was often hurt by the
laughter his work provoked.

Paul Cézanne
BOY IN A RED VEST, 1893-95
Mr. and Mrs. Paul Mellon, Upperville, VA (35x28 in.)

Although rejected from art school, Cézanne committed to painting at age 23. His work was not accepted by the Salon until he was 43. By age 50, success was slowly coming his way.

Georges Seurat
BATHERS, ASNIERES, 1883-84
The National Gallery, London (79x118 in.)

This was the first of Seurat's great large pictures. He and Signac were attempting to develop a more rational, scientific approach to making art.

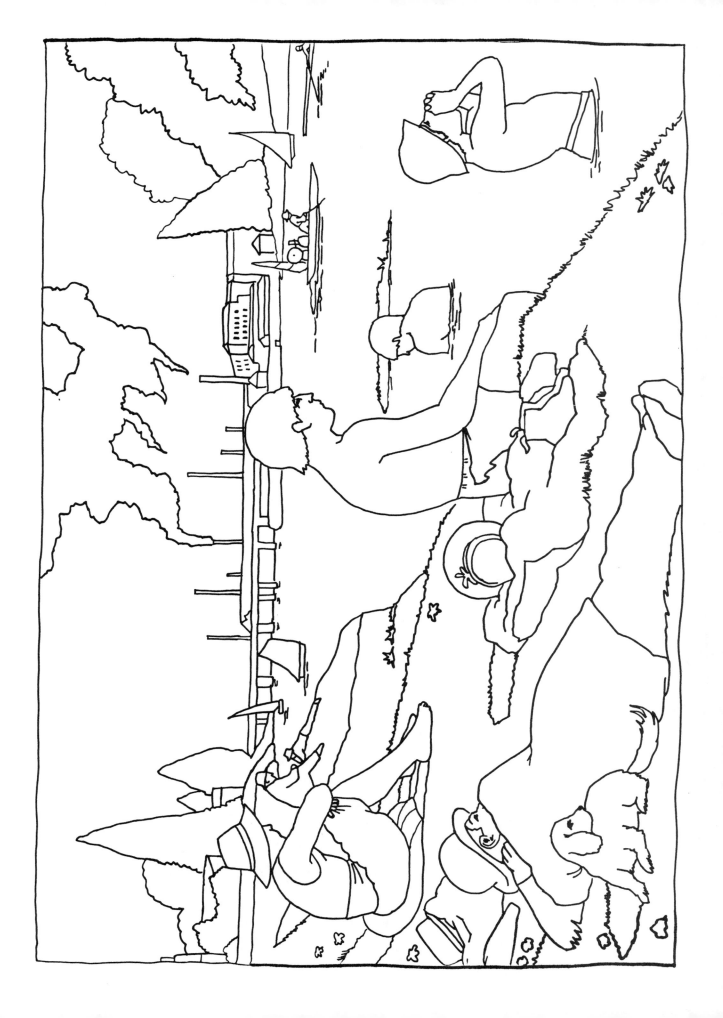

Georges Seurat
A SUNDAY AFTERNOON ON THE ISLAND
OF LA GRAND JATTE, 1884-85
Chicago Institute of Art (81x121 in.)

Seurat worked very slowly. This painting took two years, 30 color studies and 27
preliminary drawings to complete. Then it was greeted with abuse by the public
and the critics.

Georges Seurat
THE CIRCUS, 1891
Musee d'Orsay, Paris (72x60 in.)

This work was unfinished at the time of Seurat's sudden death from influenza at age 32. At that time, critics maintained he had not left one single work of lasting importance.

Paul Signac
WOMAN DOING HER HAIR, 1892
Ginette Signac Collection, Paris (24x29 in.)

Enthusiastic, impetuous and hearty, Signac was the driving force of the "Divisionists," who painted with tiny dots of color which would be "mixed" within the viewer's eye.

Paul Signac
BOULEVARD DE CLICHY IN PARIS, 1886
Minneapolis Institute of Art (18x25 in.)

The son of well-to-do parents, Signac traveled to every port from Holland to Constantinople, painting vibrant watercolors at every stop. He was the last of the group to die, in 1935.

Vincent van Gogh
CHURCH AT AUVERS
Louvre, Paris

Van Gogh failed miserably as an art dealer, teacher, bookseller, and missionary before taking up painting at age 27. He was supported his entire life by his brother, Theo.

Vincent van Gogh
THE NIGHT CAFE, 1888
Yale University Art Gallery, New Haven (38x35 in.)

For three months in 1888, van Gogh and Gauguin lived, painted and squabbled together in Arles. Supposedly, not a single van Gogh painting was sold in his lifetime.

Vincent van Gogh
BEDROOM AT ARLES
Louvre, Paris

In Arles, Van Gogh painted 200 canvases in 15 months. The villagers dubbed him "the mad painter" and soon afterward he was hospitalized in an asylum for the insane.

Vincent van Gogh
PORTRAIT OF PERE TANGUY, 1887
Stavros S. Niarchos Collection, London (25x19 in.)

Van Gogh continued to paint unmistakably disturbed pictures to the end. On a
summer Sunday in 1891, Vincent shot himself in the stomach. He died two days
later in his brother's arms.

Paul Gauguin
THE VISION AFTER THE SERMON, 1888
National Gallery of Scotland, Edinburgh (29x36 in.)

Gauguin abandoned his wife, his family, his health, his wealth, and his country in order to pursue painting. At age 55 he died alone in misery and poverty in Tahiti.

Paul Gauguin
STILL LIFE WITH THREE PUPPIES, 1888
Museum of Modern Art, New York (36x25 in.)

When Gauguin left his bank job to pursue art, his mentor Pissarro wrote "that after 30 years of painting. . .I'm flat broke. These young people should remember that!"

Henri de Toulouse-Lautrec
QUADRILLE AT THE MOULIN-ROUGE, 1892
National Gallery of Art, Washington, D.C. (32x24 in.)

The growth of Toulouse-Lautrec's legs was stunted by two successive falls as a child. At 18, he left his aristocratic family to discover the Parisian nightlife, where social outcasts like himself were most welcome.

Henri de Toulouse-Lautrec
JOCKEY GOING TO THE POST, 1899
Lithograph

Terribly obsessive, Toulouse-Lautrec was sent to a mental hospital in 1899 to recover from alcoholism. Struck by paralysis at 37, he died in his mother's arms at his boyhood home.